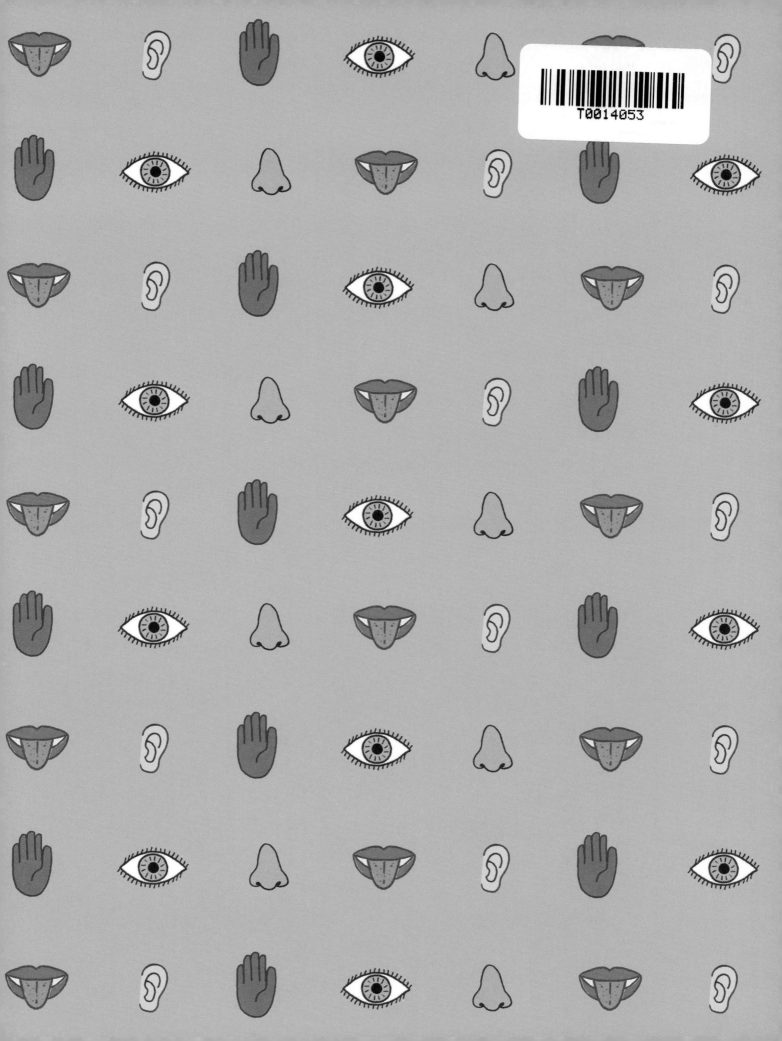

THE BRAINIAC'S BOOK OF THE

BODY AND BRAIN

Hello there Brainiac!
My name is Skully Boneapart.
I've got the inside info on your insides.
Stick with me and you'll soon be able
to rattle off some unbelievable facts
about your amazing body and brain.
Come on, don't be a lazy bones!

THE BRAINIAC'S BOOK OF THE

BODY AND BRAIN

WRITTEN BY
ROSIE COOPER

ILLUSTRATED BY
HARRIET RUSSELL

WHAT'S INSIDE?

WE ARE ALL DIFFERENT

MARVELLOUS MEDICINE

EVOLVING BODIES

WEIRD SCIENCE

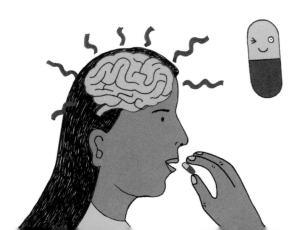

YOU OWN AN AMAZING MACHINE

YOUR BODY AND BRAIN WILL LAST A LIFETIME AND THEY'RE ONE OF A KIND

Your body and brain are the most **COMPLICATED** and **UNIQUE** things you will ever own. Millions of parts work together around the clock to keep you ticking.

BUSY BODY

While you go about your day, your body takes care of essential tasks like digesting food, getting rid of waste, keeping you at the right temperature, and fighting off infections.

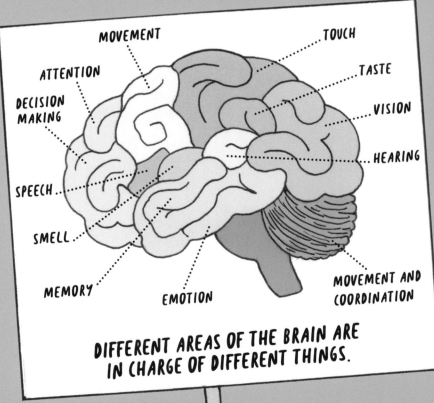

MOVEMENT
ATTENTION
DECISION MAKING
SPEECH
SMELL
MEMORY
TOUCH
TASTE
VISION
HEARING
EMOTION
MOVEMENT AND COORDINATION

DIFFERENT AREAS OF THE BRAIN ARE IN CHARGE OF DIFFERENT THINGS.

BRAIN POWER

It's hard to believe that the wrinkly gray jelly in your head is like a super computer. This is where **THOUGHTS, MEMORIES,** and **EMOTIONS** are handled. The brain is also the control center for your **SENSES.**

GUESS WHAT?
YOUR HAVE UP TO 80,000 THOUGHTS A DAY!

INSTANT MESSAGES

Super-fast signals travel from every part of your body to your brain along **NERVES**. Your brain reads the signals and you feel **SENSATIONS** like hunger, or in this case pain!

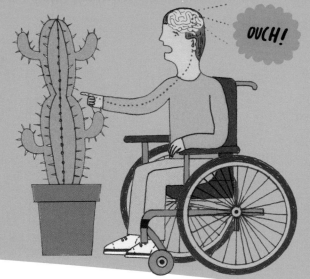

OUCH!

HEAD-TO-TOE EMOTIONS

Your body and brain are connected in all sorts of ways.
EMOTIONS are often felt in different parts of the body.

HIGHEST SENSATION

A LOT OF SENSATION

NORMAL SENSATION

LOW SENSATION

ANGER

WORRY

LOVE

HAPPINESS

SADNESS

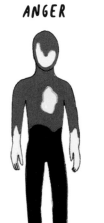

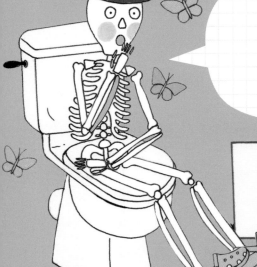

I don't know about you, but I blush when I'm **EMBARRASSED,** and I feel butterflies in my stomach when I'm **NERVOUS**. Where do you sense different emotions?

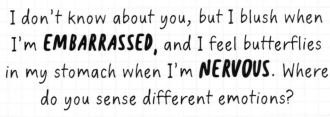

OK, IT'S TIME TO LIFT THE LID AND EXPLORE THE CURIOSITIES OF YOUR BODY AND BRAIN!

YOUR BRAIN IS A CONSTRUCTION SIT

YOU ARE A CONSTRUCTION WORKER IN CHARGE OF NEW ROUTES

BUILDING ROUTES

Every time you learn something new, construction work starts in your brain. A route, or pathway, has to be made to connect the tiny brain cells, called **NEURONS**, that carry messages to different areas.

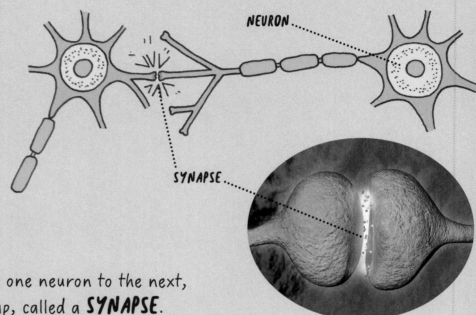

NEURON

SYNAPSE

The messages have to move from one neuron to the next, but each cell is separated by a gap, called a **SYNAPSE**.

MIND THE GAP

At first, it takes a big effort to transfer messages between neurons.

NOT ANOTHER GAP!

IT WILL BE WORTH IT.

The first time you do something new, you find it hard. The brain has to transfer messages across lots of gaps.

Keep repeating the task and a route starts to form in your brain. Messages can travel more easily.

LET'S GROW!

Your brain can keep learning new things your whole life. You can do anything you set your mind to, if you work at it. Thinking like this is called having a **GROWTH MINDSET**.

Struggling with something new? Try speaking **"YETI"**

> I CAN'T DO THAT <u>YET</u>

> I DON'T KNOW THAT <u>YET</u>

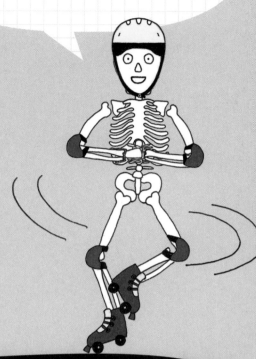

> You can learn anything, no matter how tricky. It just takes time for your neurons to build the route in your brain. Look at me! I can roller-skate now!

> THIS MAKES LIFE EASIER!

The more you go over the thing you are learning, the faster and stronger the route becomes. Soon the new thing is easy!

BROKEN BRIDGES

As well as building routes, you can break them down too.

> DANGER! WEAK BRIDGE

If you don't keep practicing the new thing, the route can get weaker. Keep the route open by going over it regularly.

TRY THIS

MY HEAD HAS BEEN HIJACKED!

FEAR AND BIG FEELINGS CAN TRIGGER A BRAIN TAKEOVER

BRAINIAC HACK: FEELING FEAR

If you are in danger, there's no time to think. Your brain switches to "emergency mode".

EMERGENCY MODE

The main part of the brain that deals with feelings, including fear, is the **AMYGDALA**. It helps keep us safe when there is a threat.

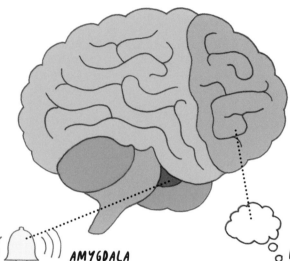

AMYGDALA

THINKING MODE

The main thinking part of the brain is the **PREFRONTAL CORTEX**. It allows us to solve problems and think calmly and logically.

PRE-FRONTAL CORTEX

SOUND THE ALARM!

The amygdala is an built-in alarm. When it senses danger it sends urgent signals to make us react quickly and without thinking.

RUN!

FREEZE!

FALSE ALARM!

Emotions like anger and worry can trigger the amygdala. Even though you are not in danger, it can bring on the same reaction as a real emergency. This is called the **AMYGDALA HIJACK**.

HIDE!

FIGHT!

BLOW UP THE ZOMBIES!

GRRRR!

KABOOM!

If **BIG EMOTIONS** take over, try these exercises to switch off **"EMERGENCY MODE."**

BREATHE DEEPLY

- Take a long, slow breath in through your nose, then breath out slowly through your mouth.

- Imagine you are blowing big bubbles through a bubble wand, or blowing seeds off a dandelion.

- Repeat for five breaths, or until you feel calm.

EXPLANATION:

When we are anxious, we take quick, shallow breaths. Deep breathing makes the heart beat more slowly and fills the body with lots of oxygen. It also tricks our brain into thinking we are calm and the amygdala alarm is switched off.

WORK IT OUT

- Think of five different animals and then put them in alphabetical order.

- Think of three friends or family members. Add up their ages.

$$8 + 4 + 11 =$$

EXPLANATION:

The prefrontal cortex loves to figure things out. Giving it tasks to do switches your brain into "thinking mode." Can you help me finish this sudoku?

FLIP FORWARD >>>
to page 62 for the **ANSWERS**

DRIFT OFF TO DREAMLAND

CLOSE YOUR EYES AND FLOAT AWAY TO A FANTASY WORLD!

NEED-TO-KNOW FACTS

In total, we **DREAM** for about two hours a night. Scientists think dreaming is the brain's way of **CLEANING UP**. It sorts through thoughts and emotions, ready to start fresh the next day.

We go through cycles of light sleep and deep sleep throughout the night. Our most **VIVID DREAMS** happen during **REM** (rapid eye movement) sleep.

IN REM SLEEP OUR EYES DART BACK AND FORTH UNDER OUR EYELIDS

DOGS DREAM TOO, BUT WE CAN ONLY GUESS WHAT ABOUT!

Scientists believe we are looking around our dreamworld during REM sleep.

When we are in REM sleep, the brain **BLOCKS MOVEMENT** in our main muscles. This stops us from acting out dreams and hurting ourselves.

Have you ever had a dream where you knew you were dreaming? This is called **LUCID DREAMING**. Some lucid dreamers can choose what happens next!

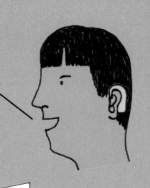

HALF ASLEEP
OUR SLEEP-WAKE CYCLE SOMETIMES GETS GLITCHES . . .

HA, HA! STOP TICKLING ME!

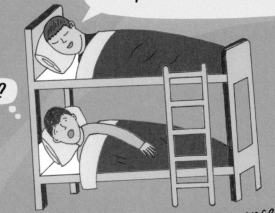

SLEEP TALKERS might talk nonsense, say random words, or even have conversations. They usually have no memory of it when they wake up!

ZZZZ

When people **SLEEPWALK,** their body is awake but their mind is still asleep. They often do everyday things in an odd way.

SLEEP PARALYSIS is when the mind wakes up but the muscles are still frozen. For a few minutes it's impossible to move or speak — like being under a spooky spell!

When Dolphins sleep they close one eye and rest half their brain. The other half stays alert so the dolphin can keep swimming and looking out for danger.

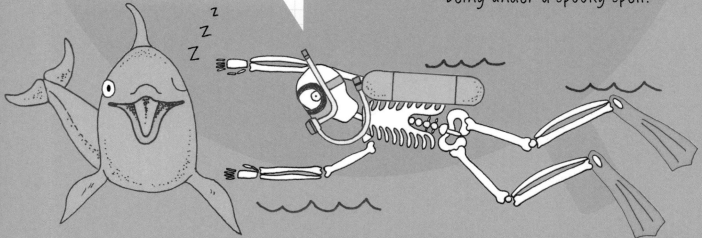

REMEMBER, REMEMBER

DO YOU HAVE A GOOD MEMORY, OR IS YOUR BRAIN PLAYING TRICKS?

BRAINIAC HACK: MEMORY

Your memory can recall so much, from friends' names, to how to walk and talk.

The brain **STORES** information and helps retrieve it again later.

The brain **FORGETS** information that it no longer needs. This clears space for new information.

The brain also **MISFILES** things, forgetting stuff we need, and remembering things we don't need or want!

Our memories are like **JIGSAWS** with **MISSING PIECES**.
We put them together, filling in the holes as best we can.

THE LONGER WE WAIT TO RETRIEVE A MEMORY THE MORE PIECES GO MISSING.

SOMETIMES OUR BRAIN MUDDLES MEMORIES, CHANGING DETAILS, PEOPLE, AND PLACES.

WE MIGHT THINK WE REMEMBER AN EVENT THAT WE HAVE BEEN TOLD ABOUT OR SEEN IN PHOTOS.

My first teacher

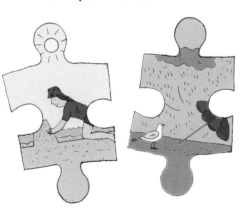

My best vacation

My first birthday

14

MEMORY GAME

TRY THIS

Grab a pen and paper and a stopwatch or timer.
Look at the 12 objects below for 15 seconds.
Close the book and write down everything you saw.
Check to see how many you remembered.

MEMORIZATION
IS AN OFFICIAL SPORT.
TOP COMPETITORS CAN REMEMBER
THE ORDER OF A PACK OF SHUFFLED
PLAYING CARDS IN UNDER 15 SECONDS!

EXPLANATION:
You will probably forget quite a few objects
the first time you try. Repeat the activity a few
more times and you will remember more and more.
This is because repetition allows your brain
to file the information in your memory.

MAKING SENSE OF THE WORLD

YOUR SENSES BOMBARD YOUR HARDWORKING BRAIN WITH MESSAGES

BRAINIAC HACK: SENSES TEAMWORK

NERVES in the eyes, ears, nose, tongue, and skin send messages to the brain, allowing us to see, hear, smell, taste, and feel touch. **SENSORY NERVES** around the body connect to the **SPINAL CORD**, which carries messages to the brain.

Our senses often **WORK TOGETHER** to help our brain make sense of the information it is receiving.

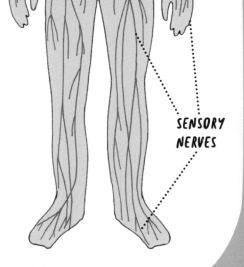

BRAIN

SPINAL CORD

SENSORY NERVES

SENSORY NERVES

SEE STEAM AND HEAR SIZZLING — IT'S HOT.

SMELLS GOOD. MOUTH IS WATERING.

IT LOOKS LIKE APPLE PIE. IT TASTES LIKE APPLE PIE.

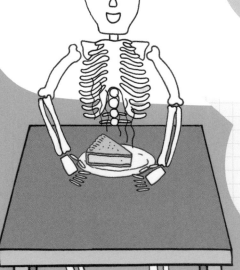

Mmm! My senses are telling me this is definitely apple pie. Sometimes our senses disagree and give different information. Try these activities to see this in action.

TEST YOUR SENSES

 How food **LOOKS** can affect how it **TASTES**.

TRY THIS: Put apple juice in three numbered cups. Add red food coloring to cup 1, orange to cup 2, and green to cup 3. Ask a volunteer to sip each one and say what it tastes like. Do they think there's a difference? Now try the activity with three different flavors dyed the same color!

 We can't **TASTE** properly without our sense of **SMELL**.

TRY THIS: Ask a volunteer to close their eyes and pinch their nose. Offer them different-flavored ice pops or ice cream to lick one at a time. Can they identify them? Ask them to repeat the activity with their nose unpinched. Do they find it easier to taste the flavors?

 How good is our sense of **TOUCH** without our **SIGHT**?

THIS FEELS REALLY SOFT.

TRY THIS: Find a few interesting-shaped or textured objects such as dried pasta, coins, toys, or dried fruit. Place them in a bag. Ask a volunteer to feel each object and guess what it is. How many do they get right?

IF WE LOSE OUR SIGHT, THE BRAIN CONCENTRATES ON THE MESSAGES COMING FROM THE OTHER SENSES. BLIND PEOPLE RELY ON HEARING AND TOUCH MORE THAN SIGHTED PEOPLE.

SUPER SENSES

YOU ARE USING ALL SORTS OF SENSES YOU NEVER KNEW YOU HAD!

SECRET SENSES

As well as sight, hearing, touch, smell, and taste, we have some extra senses that keep us moving. Here are a few of them . . .

CHRONOCEPTION
Our sense of time passing.

INTEROCEPTION
Our sense of what is happening inside the body. It lets us know when we are hungry, thirsty, hot, cold, or tired.

EQUILIBRIOCEPTION
Information from our ears, eyes, and movement sensors help us balance.

WOAH! STEADY!

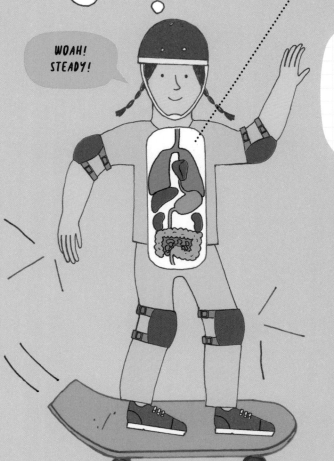

Interoception is what lets us know when we need to go to the bathroom too!

PROPRIOCEPTION
Our sense of where each part of our body is. It allows us to eat without missing our lips—or skateboard without looking at our feet!

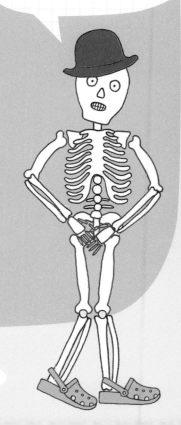

 FLIP FORWARD >>> to page 56 for more information about PROPRIOCEPTION

SENSES SUPERPOWER

CAN YOU TASTE A COLOR OR FEEL A SMELL?

If the answer is yes, then you might have **SYNESTHESIA**.
This is when the brain **LINKS** two or more unconnected **SENSES**
together. Only one out of every twenty-five people has synesthesia.
Often they are born with it, so it feels totally normal to them.

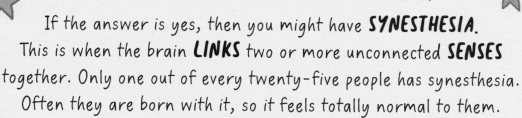

HEARING a word might fill your mouth with a certain **FLAVOR**. "Morning" might taste like honey or burned toast!

Every **COLOR** might have its own **TASTE**. Imagine what flavor a rainbow could be!

Certain **SMELLS** might give you a physical **FEELING**. Sniffing bonfire smoke might feel like being stroked with a feather.

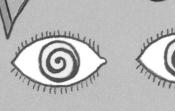

Hearing **MUSIC** might trigger a swirl of moving **COLORS** before your eyes.

GUESS WHAT?
MUSICIANS BILLIE EILISH AND PHARRELL WILLIAMS BOTH HAVE SYNESTHESIA.

WHY DO I FEEL DIZZY?

IT'S ALL DOWN TO SLOSHY CANALS AND TINY TICKLED HAIRS!

WOBBLE!

WOBBLE!

NEED-TO-KNOW FACTS

When you spin around and stop quickly, you lose your balance or feel dizzy. This **DIZZY FEELING** is because a part of you is still moving!

Your inner ear has three fluid-filled tubes, called **SEMI-CIRCULAR CANALS**. As you move, the fluid sloshes around moving jelly-like blobs that contain **TINY HAIRS**. This tells your brain, "Hey, you're moving!" When you feel dizzy, it's because the fluid in your ears is still **SLOSHING**, even though your body is **STILL**.

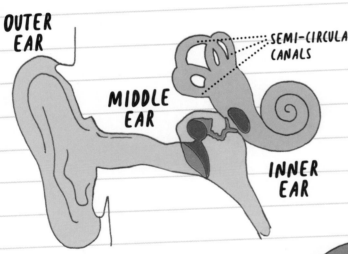

OUTER EAR

SEMI-CIRCULAR CANALS

MIDDLE EAR

INNER EAR

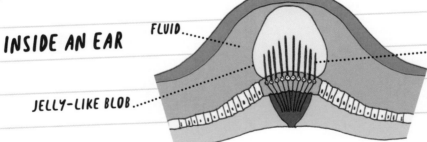

INSIDE AN EAR

FLUID

TINY HAIRS MOVE

JELLY-LIKE BLOB

TRY THIS

WHIRLING WATER

Half-fill a glass with water. Move the glass in a circle to make the water swirl, then put the glass down.
The water keep swirling even though the glass is still— just like the fluid in your ears when you stop spinning!

WHAT'S A DANCER'S FAVORITE VEGETABLE?

SPIN-ACH!

MOTION COMMOTION

If you read a book during a twisty car trip, you might get **MOTION SICKNESS**. This is because your brain gets confused about whether you are moving or still. Your inner ear tells your brain, "You're moving!" but your eyes tell it, "You are still!" Looking at the passing scenery helps your brain sort out the messages.

Astronauts often get **SPACE MOTION SICKNESS**. The low gravity in space means the fluid in their ear canals does not slosh around in the normal way. As astronauts float upside down in their spacecraft, their inner ear can't sense motion, but their eyes tell the brain, "You are definitely moving!"

In ancient China, doctors recommended drinking urine (pee) to help with motion sickness caused by riding in wobbly sedan chairs. I think I'd rather be sick!

NOW YOU SEE IT . . . NOW YOU DON'T

THE WEIRD WIRING THAT MAKES EVERYONE A TINY BIT BLIND

BRAINIAC HACK: BLIND SPOT

Humans (and all creatures with a backbone) have eyes that are "wired" back-to-front!

The back of your eye has millions of **PHOTORECEPTOR CELLS**. They turn light rays into signals that the brain can understand. Tiny **NERVE FIBERS** carry the signals to the brain.

The problem is, the nerve fibers run in front of the photoreceptor cells.

Where the nerves meet at the back of the eye there is a gap with no photoreceptor cells. This causes a **BLIND SPOT**.

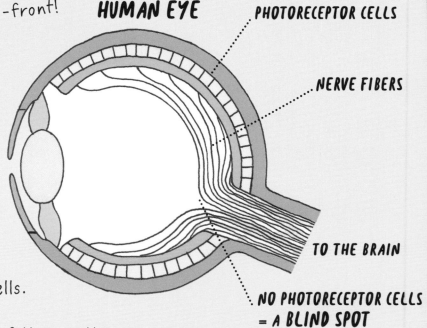

HUMAN EYE

PHOTORECEPTOR CELLS

NERVE FIBERS

TO THE BRAIN

NO PHOTORECEPTOR CELLS = A BLIND SPOT

SPOT THE DIFFERENCE

Cephalopods (sea creatures such as octopus and squid) are "wired" differently. Their nerve fibers run behind their photoreceptor cells—so no blind spot!

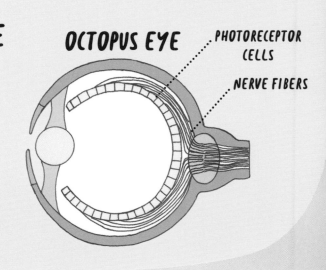

OCTOPUS EYE

PHOTORECEPTOR CELLS

NERVE FIBERS

TRY THIS

VANISHING ACT

Find your blind spot and make the rabbit vanish into thin air!

1. Hold the book at arm's length.

2. Cover your RIGHT eye. Look at the magician with your LEFT eye.

3. Slowly move the book nearer to you.

4. At some point the rabbit will disappear.

5. Now cover the LEFT eye and look at the rabbit with your RIGHT eye to make the magician disappear.

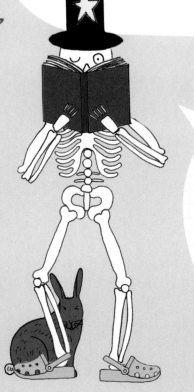

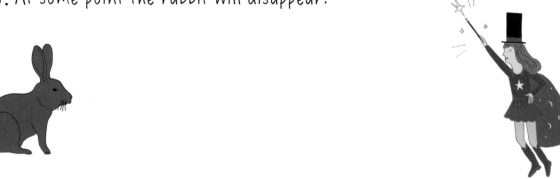
When you have both eyes open you don't notice your blind spots because your eyes help each other out. Even with one eye closed, you need to get the image in just the right place or your brain fills in the missing bits of the image.

DATA DUMP

BATHTUBS OF SWEAT

ALL SORTS OF SUBSTANCES ARE CONSTANTLY OOZING, DRIPPING, AND SQUEEZING.

By the time you are 10 years old, your body factory will produce:

4.5 KG

9.9 LBS OF DEAD SKIN CELLS
(the same weight as a bouncing newborn baby)

ALMOST A GALLON OF TEARS
(enough to fill almost 9 cans of soda)

2,500 LBS OF POOP
(as heavy as 100 cats)

1,300 GALLONS OF MUCUS (SNOT)
(enough to fill the fuel tank of an average car 80 times)

900 GALLONS OF FARTS
(enough to fill an elevator)

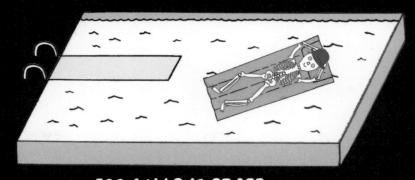

500 GALLONS OF PEE
(enough to fill a small swimming pool)

No one has ever measured it, but the body makes a lot of earwax too. Earwax isn't wax at all, but a mix of fat, dead skin cells, sweat, and dirt. It also contains acid for killing germs, which is why it tastes so horrible! YUCK!

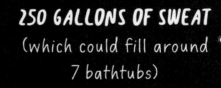

250 GALLONS OF SWEAT
(which could fill around 7 bathtubs)

120 INCHES OF FINGERNAIL (around ten inches for each nail)

LEAKS AND DRIPS

WHAT IS ALL THE SNOTTY, WEEPY, DRIBBLY STUFF FOR?

NOSE

ARMIES OF SNOT

The slimy stuff up your nose is called **MUCUS**. It is a gooey security guard protecting all the paths in and out of your body.

1. Every breath we take might contain **DUST**, **DIRT**, or **GERMS**. The mucus in your nose helps to trap these invaders.

2. We cough or sneeze out mucus containing germs and dust.

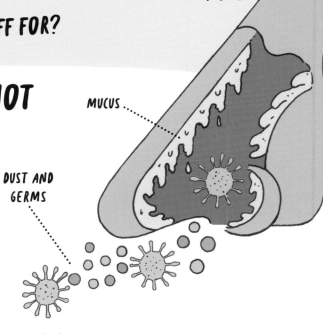

MUCUS

DUST AND GERMS

3. Most of the mucus gets swallowed. It travels to the **STOMACH**, where germs are killed.

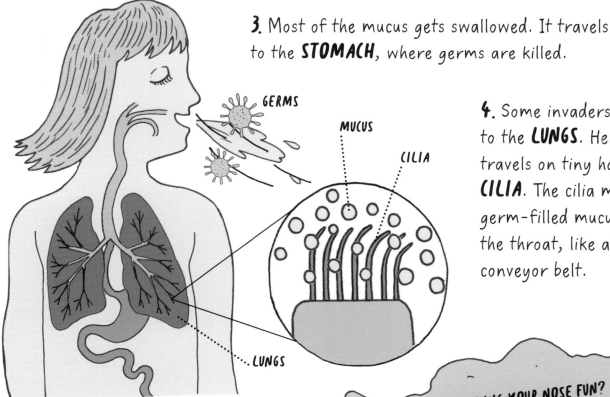

GERMS

MUCUS

CILIA

4. Some invaders make it to the **LUNGS**. Here, mucus travels on tiny hairs called **CILIA**. The cilia move the germ-filled mucus back up the throat, like a sticky conveyor belt.

LUNGS

GUESS WHAT?
THE SCIENTIFIC NAME FOR A SEVERE CASE OF NOSE PICKING IS RHINOTILLEXOMANIA!

IS PICKING YOUR NOSE FUN? YES! IS IT OK TO DO IT? SADLY, NO. PICKING YOUR NOSE CAN SPREAD GERMS.

OVERFLOWING DRAINS

Our eyes make tiny tears nonstop. This salty liquid
keeps our eyes moist, clean and germ-free.

TEARS ARE MADE
IN A GLAND ABOVE
EACH EYE.

BLINKING PUSHES
TEAR LIQUID
ACROSS OUR EYES.

THE LIQUID DRAINS
INTO TWO SMALL
HOLES AT THE TOP
AND BOTTOM LID
OF EACH EYE.

THE LIQUID FLOWS DOWN
TUBES IN THE NOSE AND
IS SWALLOWED.

SO, WHY ARE YOU CRYING?

Our eyes make three different
kinds of tears, depending on
what they are needed for.

Dry eyes?
BASAL TEARS
keep them moist.

This book is a real tearjerker.
When we cry there is so much
liquid, tears spill out of our eyes
and our nose drains overflow.
Our nose is leaking tears!
Sniff!

Crying with laughter,
sadness, or pain?
PSYCHIC TEARS contain
a painkiller that makes
us feel better.

Something
scratchy in your eye?
REFLEX TEARS wash
away gross stuff.

TRAVELING POOP

FROM THE MOMENT YOU GULP, YOUR FOOD IS ON THE MOVE.

WHAT'S IN A POOP?

MUCUS

GREEN BILE
AND OLD RED BLOOD CELLS
(MAKES POOP BROWN)

BACTERIA (MAKES POOP SMELL)

FIBER (UNDIGESTABLE FOOD)

WASTE-MAKING MACHINE

Your **DIGESTIVE SYSTEM** is a long tube that stretches from your **ESOPHAGUS** to your **RECTUM** (bottom). If unraveled, it would measure over **26 FEET** — that's twice as long as an average car!

ESOPHAGUS

THE LIVER MAKES
DIGESTIVE JUICES

FOOD IS CHURNED
WITH DIGESTIVE JUICES
IN THE STOMACH

THE SMALL
INTESTINE ABSORBS
THE GOODNESS
FROM FOOD

THE LARGE INTESTINE
EXTRACTS WATER
FROM FOOD, AND
TURNS THE WASTE
INTO LUMPS OF POOP

RECTUM

Those **GURGLING SOUNDS** are food being churned, mashed, and squeezed by the muscly walls of your digestive system. They are called **BORBORYGMI.**

GURGLE!
GURGLE!

It takes **ONE** to **THREE DAYS** to make poop. Your body absorbs carbohydrates, protein, fats, and vitamins from food and gets rid of **FIBER** (undigestable food).

RATE YOUR POOP

The Bristol Stool Scale groups poop
into seven types. Which poop looks like yours?

TYPE 7
SLOPPY LIKE GRAVY

TYPE 1
HARD LIKE RABBIT DROPPINGS

TYPE 6
MUSHY LIKE OATMEAL

TYPE 2
LUMPY LIKE A
BUNCH OF GRAPES

TYPE 5
LIKE SOFT CHICKEN NUGGETS

TYPE 3
LIKE CORN ON THE COB

TYPE 4
LIKE A SAUSAGE

TYPES 1 OR 2
YOU HAVE CONSTIPATION
(YOU FIND IT HARD TO POOP)

TYPES 6 OR 7
YOU HAVE DIARRHEA (YOUR POOP IS TOO
RUNNY AND YOU GO TOO OFTEN)

TYPE 3, 4 OR 5
IT'S THE PERFECT POOP!

YOU CAN IMPROVE
YOUR POOP SCORE
BY EATING A WELL-BALANCED
DIET WITH LOTS OF
FRUITS, VEGGIES, AND
WHOLEGRAIN FOODS.

TRY
THIS

POOPCORN EXPERIMENT

Your body can't digest the
outside of a corn kernel.
This makes corn perfect for
tracking your food's journey
through your body.

1. Eat some sweetcorn and
write down the day and time.
2. Look out for the yellow corn
kernels in the toilet when you poop.
3. Write down the time and date
you spy the corn, then work out
how long it took.

MAKE FRIENDS WITH FARTS

FARTS ARE FUNNY, NOISY, AND NORMAL, BUT WHY DO WE MAKE STINKY GAS?

NEED-TO-KNOW FACTS

Most people produce between 10 and 20 farts a day. Follow the making of a fart . . .

1. When we eat, we also **SWALLOW AIR**. We burp out some of the air. The rest ends up on a trip through our digestive system.

BURP!

2. The stomach and the small intestine can't digest some **CARBOHYDRATES** so they travel to the **LARGE INTESTINE**.

............STOMACH

.........SMALL INTESTINE

3. In the large intestine, millions of microscopic **GUT BACTERIA** feast on the hard-to-digest food, which creates **GAS**.

4. The bubbles of gas make their way through the wiggly tube of the large intestine until they are released out of the rectum (bottom).

LARGE INTESTINE.........

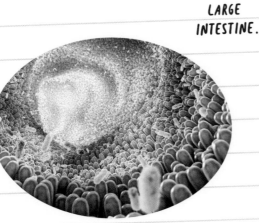

GUT BACTERIA

PARP!

ONLY 1% OF A FART IS SMELLY GAS. THE STINKY INGREDIENT IS

HYDROGEN SULPHIDE — THE SAME STUFF THAT GIVES ROTTEN EGGS THEIR WHIFF.

WHY SHOULD YOU NEVER FART IN AN ELEVATOR?

IT'S WRONG ON SO MANY LEVELS.

FARTY FACTS

FART JARS

In the Middle Ages, doctors advised keeping farts in jars as a plague preventative. The idea was that if the plague came to town you could take a whiff to protect yourself.

FLYING FARTS

In 2015, a plane had to make an emergency landing when the farts of 2,186 goats in the cargo hold set off the smoke alarms. The sensors confused the farts with smoke fumes.

PROFESSIONAL FARTER

French entertainer Joseph Pujol (1857-1945) could pull in air through his butt and then blow it out to play the flute, blow out candles, and make thunderstorm sound effects.

Foods that make smelly farts include beans, onions, broccoli, cabbage, cauliflower, and eggs. I NEVER fart. It's not that I'm embarrassed, I just don't have the guts!

31

WE ARE ALL DIFFERENT

ALL KINDS OF BRAINS

WE ARE NOT ALL THE SAME, SO IT'S GOOD TO UNDERSTAND HOW WE ARE DIFFERENT.

Human bodies are not all the same, and neither are human brains. This is called **NEURODIVERSITY**. It describes the many ways we think, learn, communicate, and experience the world.

Being **NEURODIVERGENT** might mean you have your own way of expressing yourself and interacting with others.

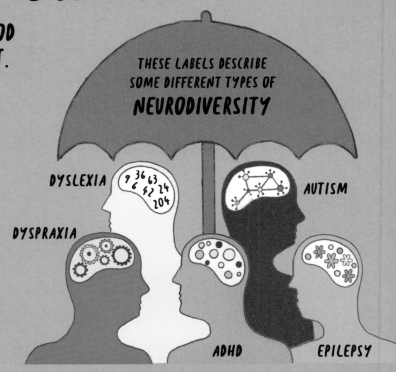

THESE LABELS DESCRIBE SOME DIFFERENT TYPES OF **NEURODIVERSITY**

DYSLEXIA

AUTISM

DYSPRAXIA

ADHD

EPILEPSY

A LITTLE OR A LOT?

If your senses take in a lot of information, you might be **SENSORY AVOIDANT**.
If your senses take in less information, you might be **SENSORY SEEKING**.

SENSORY AVOIDANT PEOPLE MIGHT ...

- STRUGGLE WITH LOUD NOISES
- FIND THE TEXTURE OF SOME FOODS UNPLEASANT
- FIND LABELS OR CLOTHING SCRATCHY AND ITCHY
- PREFER CALM, UNCROWDED PLACES

SENSORY SEEKING PEOPLE MIGHT ...

- LOOK FOR THINGS TO TOUCH, HEAR, OR TASTE
- LIKE BRIGHT COLORS AND LIGHTS
- NOTICE PAIN LESS THAN OTHER PEOPLE
- LOVE SPINNING AND RUNNING AROUND

HAPPY OR SAD?

If you're neurodivergent, you might not **SHOW EMOTIONS** in a typical way. Or you might find it hard to **READ EMOTIONS** in other people.

We all get emotions confused at times. Look at these expressions and body language and pick at least **TWO WORDS** to describe each picture.

BORED	SAD
SURPRISED	SHY
TIRED	EXCITED
SUSPICIOUS	SCARED

FAIR OR EQUAL?

Neurodivergent people might need **EXTRA HELP**, such as more time to do schoolwork, breaks from class, or support to calm their emotions.

Giving these children the same-sized box is **EQUAL**, but is it fair?

It's **FAIR** to treat people according to what they need.

Would you like to make friends with a neurodivergent classmate? Here are a few things to try . . .

MY FRIENDSHIP TIPS

COMMUNICATE IN A WAY THAT WORKS FOR THEM. (THIS COULD BE ON A TABLET OR DEVICE.)

FIND OUT WHAT THEY'RE **INTERESTED** IN AND LEARN ABOUT IT TOO.

UNDERSTAND IF THEY GET UPSET SOMETIMES. THEY MIGHT JUST BE OVERWHELMED.

FLIP FORWARD >>> to page 62 for the **ANSWERS**

WE ARE ALL DIFFERENT

GENDER COOKIES

HUMANS ARE A LOT LIKE COOKIES

There are a squillion different cookie flavors, and they all taste unique because of their ingredients. People are a combination of "ingredients," too. Check out the **GENDERBREAD PERSON**.

ATTRACTION

Who we are drawn to. Our special someones (or no-ones!)

GENDER IDENTITY

How we see ourselves, based on what we feel inside, our personality, and our likes and dislikes.

GENDER EXPRESSION

How we present ourselves to the world, through our hairstyle, clothing, words, actions, and hobbies.

SEX

What it is decided we are at birth, based on our genitals. We can be male, female, or intersex (a mixture of both).

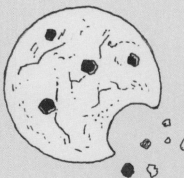

34

FLIP FORWARD >>> to the Glossary on page 60 for more **GENDER WORDS**

Everyone's **GENDERBREAD RECIPE** is different. There are countless combinations of gender identity, gender expression, attraction, and sex. Your own special recipe may change over your lifetime.

Many cultures sort people into two categories. This is called **GENDER BINARY** (binary means two). These categories are described as **"MALE"** and **"FEMALE,"** but humans are much more complex than that!

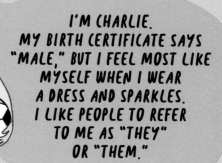

I'M CHARLIE. MY BIRTH CERTIFICATE SAYS "MALE," BUT I FEEL MOST LIKE MYSELF WHEN I WEAR A DRESS AND SPARKLES. I LIKE PEOPLE TO REFER TO ME AS "THEY" OR "THEM."

I'M KAI. I LIKE DANCING. I HAVE SHORT HAIR AND WEAR TRACKSUITS. I LOVE MOVIES STARRING TOM HOLLAND. SOMETIMES PEOPLE THINK I'M A BOY, BUT I LIKE BEING A GIRL.

Our **HOBBIES**, the **CLOTHES** we wear, who we are **ATTRACTED TO,** and who we see ourselves as aren't decided by our sex.

Until the 1940s pink was thought of as a boys' color and blue was for girls. Young children, no matter their gender, wore dresses or gowns up to the early 1900s. Fashions change! What colors and types of clothes make you feel your best?

ACCESS FOR EVERYONE

A WELL-DESIGNED WORLD IS A BETTER WORLD FOR ALL OF US

BRAINIAC HACK: DISABILITY

ONE IN FIVE people on Earth has a **DISABILITY**. This can affect how easily we do things such as see, hear, speak, move around, or learn.

WHAT TO SAY?

PERSON WITH A DISABILITY ← IF IN DOUBT, ASK THE PERSON WHICH THEY PREFER. → DISABLED PERSON

I SEE MY DISABILITY AS ONLY **ONE PART** OF WHO I AM.

I SEE MY DISABILITY AS AN **IMPORTANT PART** OF WHO I AM.

Disability is most noticeable when a neighborhood, building, or equipment is not designed for everyone to use. This is called **POOR ACCESSIBILITY**.

POOR ACCESSIBILITY

SAM LOVES WATCHING MOVIES, BUT THIS MOVIE THEATER IS NOT MAKING IT EASY FOR HER IN HER WHEELCHAIR.

GOOD ACCESSIBILITY

THIS BUILDING HAS A RAMP SO SAM CAN SEE THE MOVIE WITH HER FRIENDS.

FAIR PLAY

One of these parks has good accessibility for everyone and one does not. Which is which? Can you spot 6 differences between the scenes?

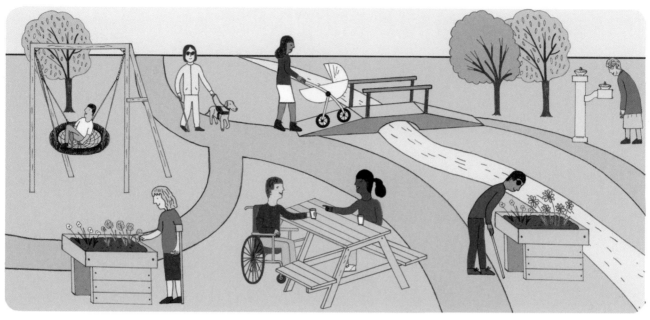

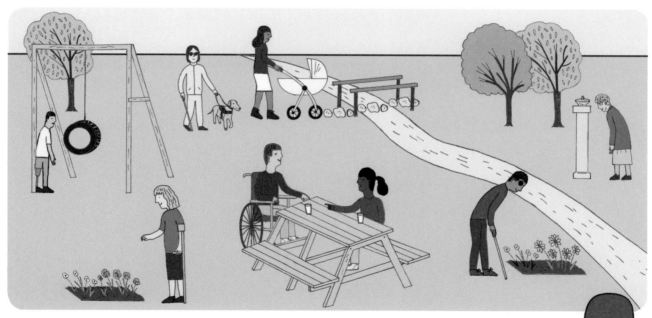

Not all disabilities are ones we can see. For instance, someone might have painful joints from arthritis, or poor balance from a head injury.

FLIP FORWARD >>> to page 62 for the ANSWERS

37

GORY INVESTIGATIONS

DATA DUMP

THE GRUESOME, SMELLY, AND DEADLY HISTORY OF DISSECTION!

Cutting open a dead body is called **DISSECTION**. It's one of the main ways people have learned about **ANATOMY** — the inside structure of the body.

LET'S TRASH THIS GRAY WRINKLY THING.

BYE BYE BRAIN!

By mummifying the dead, **ANCIENT EGYPTIANS** learned what was inside the body. All the organs were removed from the belly and chest, except the **HEART**, which was thought to be the thinking, intelligent part. The **BRAIN** was scooped out and thrown away!

THEY CALL ME THE FOUNDER OF ANATOMY.

ANCIENT GREEK GEEK

Over 2,000 years ago, **HEROPHILOS** was one of the first doctors to dissect dead bodies. He realized that the **BRAIN** is our **THINKING** part, not the heart, as previously thought.

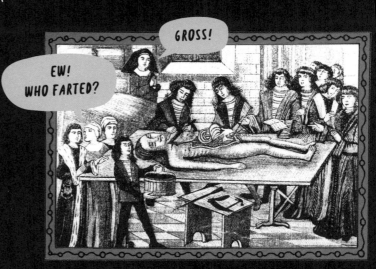

GROSS!

EW! WHO FARTED?

STINKY STUDIES

In the 1300s, European universities taught anatomy to medical students by cutting open executed criminals. There were **NO FRIDGES** to keep corpses cool, so in hot weather they soon started to **STINK**!

BODY ART

In the late 1400s, some artists started taking dead bodies apart to improve their art. **LEONARDO DA VINCI** dissected over 30 corpses to see what gives the body its **SHAPE**. His drawings proved very useful to scientists.

GRAVE ROBBERS

In the 18th and 19th centuries, there was a shortage of suitable bodies for doctors to dissect. Medical schools offered good **MONEY** for a fresh corpse. This led to **BODY SNATCHERS** digging up recently buried bodies to claim the cash.

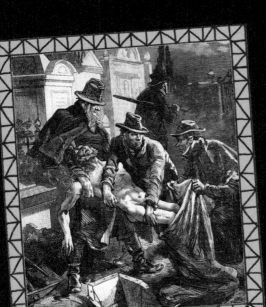

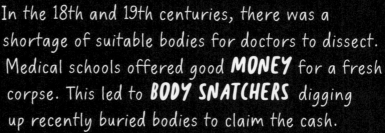

I'M HARE. I BLAME BURKE.

IT WAS ALL HARE'S IDEA.

DEADLY CRIMES

In Scotland in 1827, two men named William Burke and William Hare decided that the best way to get paid for dead bodies was to create them! They were found guilty of **16 MURDERS**!

Let me out of here! In parts of the UK, body snatching was so common that people put iron cages, called "mortsafes," around family graves to protect them.

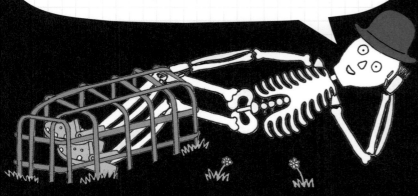

Medical students still learn about **ANATOMY** by **DISSECTING** bodies. Now bodies are donated by people who are happy to give their body to science when they die.

READY FOR YOUR CLOSE-UP?

THE ULTIMATE SELFIES ARE PICTURES OF YOUR INSIDES!

Amazing machines look inside the human body and check for problems
— no cutting-open required!

SPY CAM

An **ENDOSCOPE** is a tool that surgeons use to view internal organs without operating. A bendy tube with a camera is pushed through the mouth, a small cut, or other opening such as the bottom.

An **ENDOSCOPE CAPSULE** is swallowed like a pill! It takes thousands of pictures on its way through the digestive system, before being pooped out.

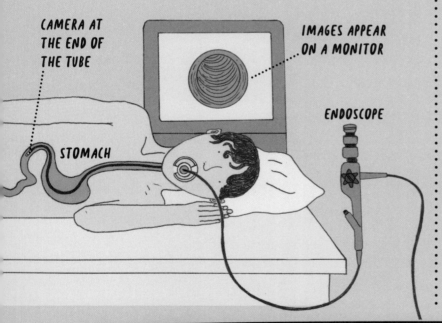

CAMERA AT THE END OF THE TUBE

IMAGES APPEAR ON A MONITOR

ENDOSCOPE

STOMACH

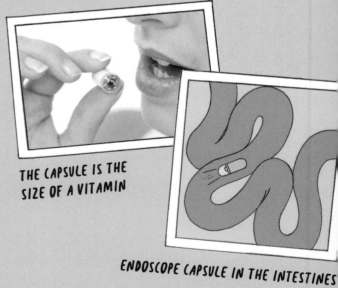

THE CAPSULE IS THE SIZE OF A VITAMIN

ENDOSCOPE CAPSULE IN THE INTESTINES

STRANGE BUT TRUE

In 1868, endoscopes were just being developed. German doctor Adolf Kussmaul had a brilliant idea that allowed him to try out the technique. He performed the first **ENDOSCOPY** on a **SWORD-SWALLOWER** who gulped down the 18.5 inch long metal tube with ease.

AMAZING RAYS

X-RAY MACHINES pass invisible rays of energy through the body to produce images. Different parts of the body block different amounts of rays.

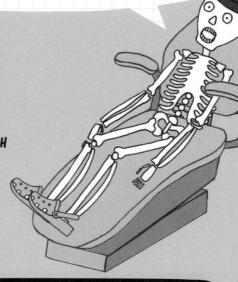

Wilhelm Röntgen discovered X-rays in 1895. He named them "X" because they were an unknown type of radiation. Too much radiation is harmful, but X-rays done by a doctor or dentist are very safe.

BONES
BLOCK X-RAYS AND APPEAR WHITE

MUSCLE, FLUID, FAT
ALL X-RAYS PASS THROUGH AND APPEAR GRAY

LUNGS FILLED WITH AIR
ALL X-RAYS PASS THROUGH AND APPEAR BLACK

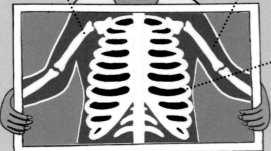

STRANGE BUT TRUE

Between the 1920s and 1960s, before the dangers of big doses of radiation were understood, shoe shops used X-rays to **FIT SHOES!** People popped their **SHOED** feet in the **FLUOROSCOPE MACHINE** to reveal the bones inside.

X-RAY TEST

LEFT   RIGHT
☐ GOOD ☐
☐ FAIR ☐
☐ POOR ☐

RIGHT WAY   WRONG WAY

INSIDE STORY

High-tech scanning machines make images of almost every part of the body, from the middle of the brain to unborn babies.

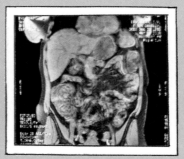

MRI SCAN OF INTERNAL ORGANS

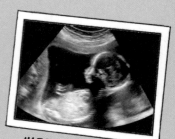

ULTRASOUND SCAN OF A BABY IN THE WOMB

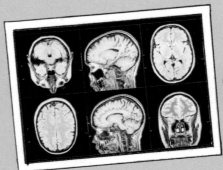

CT SCAN OF SLICES THROUGH THE BRAIN

BUG INFESTATION!

MEET THE MINI GUESTS THAT MAKE THEIR HOME IN YOUR BODY

BRAINIAC HACK: TYPES OF GERMS

The human body contains trillions of tiny **MICROORGANISMS**.

MICROORGANISMS CAN ONLY BE SEEN UNDER A MICROSCOPE

Most microorganisms are harmless, some are even helpful to the body, but a few make us sick. They are called **GERMS**, and there are four main types:

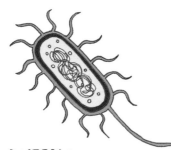

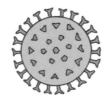

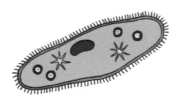

BACTERIA
CAN CAUSE EAR INFECTIONS AND SORE THROATS

VIRUSES
CAN CAUSE CHICKENPOX, COVID, AND COLDS

PROTOZOA
CAN CAUSE STOMACH ACHES AND SICKNESS

FUNGI
AN ITCHY FOOT RASH CALLED ATHLETES FOOT IS CAUSED BY A FUNGUS

We usually pick up germs through the **AIR**, by coming in close contact with an **INFECTED PERSON**, or by **TOUCHING** things they've touched.

The helpful bacteria, viruses, and fungi in your body are known as your MICROBIOME. Most live in your gut and help keep you healthy. Your microbiome weighs about the same as your brain!

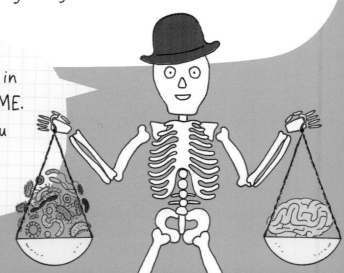

PASS IT ON . . .

TRY THIS

See how easily **GERMS SPREAD** with this experiment!

You will need:
• glitter (pretend germs) • hand lotion to help the glitter stick (pretend sweat) • a few friends or family (germ carriers)

1. Get everyone to line up and rub lotion on their hands.
2. The first person covers one hand in the glittery "germs."
3. Shake hands down the line.
How many people end up with "germy" hands?

OPERATION CLEANUP

Before the discovery of germs, people thought **BAD SMELLS**, too much **BLOOD** in the body, or **EVIL SPIRITS** caused disease!

EARLY SURGEONS operated without washing their hands and wore gowns covered in pus and guts from other patients. Many patients died from infections.

In the 1860s, scientist **LOUIS PASTEUR** proved germs existed. However, it took a while for people to understand how germs spread disease.

In the late 1860s, **JOSEPH LISTER** made surgeons wash their hands and wear clean gowns. Deaths from infections fell. Hurray!

Every time you **WASH YOUR HANDS**, you are taking part in a marvel of modern medicine!

FLIP FORWARD >>> to page 45 to find out about "BLOODLETTING"

ARE YOU POSITIVE OR NEGATIVE?

YOU PROBABLY DON'T GET ALOING WITH EVERYONE YOU MEET.
YOUR BLOOD IS THE SAME!

NEED-TO-KNOW FACTS

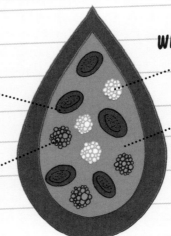

ONE DROP OF
BLOOD CONTAINS...

3 MILLION RED BLOOD
CELLS DELIVERING OXYGEN
TO YOUR WHOLE BODY

3,700
WHITE BLOOD CELLS
FIGHTING GERMS

WATERY LIQUID
CALLED PLASMA
THAT CARRIES FOOD
TO YOUR CELLS

160,000 PLATELETS THAT CLUMP
TOGETHER TO STOP CUTS FROM BLEEDING

There are different types of blood: A+, B+, O+, AB+, A-, B-, O-, AB-.
Whether blood is positive (+) or negative (-) depends on whether it
contains a certain protein or not.

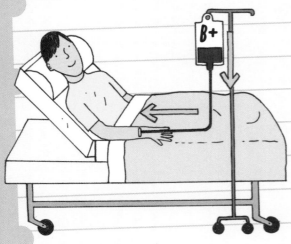

RECEIVING BLOOD

If you lose blood through an injury or surgery,
you may need a **TRANSFUSION** (when another
person's blood is added to yours so that you have
enough in your body.). Only certain blood
types will be a match for yours. Mixing bloods
that don't match can be deadly.

O- BLOOD IS THE ONLY
BLOOD TYPE THAT CAN BE
SAFELY GIVEN TO ANYONE

GIVING BLOOD

Healthy adults can **DONATE BLOOD**.
It flows out of a vein into a special bag where
it is stored. The donor's body soon makes
new blood to replace what they donated.

WHAT WAS THE RESULT OF YOUR BLOOD TEST?

I GOT AN A+ AND I DIDN'T EVEN HAVE TO STUDY!

TRANSFUSION CONFUSION

Today, getting a blood transfusion is very safe, but that wasn't always the case . . .

Before scientists discovered blood types in the early 1900s, transfusions were very hit or miss. In the first experiments in the 1600s, **ANIMAL BLOOD** was put into people.

In the late 1800s, some doctors decided to try replacing lost blood with **COW'S MILK**. This had bloodcurdling results!

Instead of giving blood, doctors used to take it out! For thousands of years, 'bloodletting' was mistakenly used as a cure for illness. Doctors made cuts or used bloodsucking leeches to get the blood out. They won't get much out of me!

In the future, you might be given blood from a wiggly **MARINE WORM**. The lugworm doesn't have a blood type so it's possible that it could be safely mixed with any human blood. Does that make you squirm?

LEFTOVER BODY PARTS

POINTLESS BUMPS AND TINY TAILS ARE CLUES TO OUR PAST!

NOTHARCTUS

Meet your ancient relative, Notharctus. It looked like a lemur and swung from trees 45 million years ago! Humans have come a long way since then, but we have been left with some parts from our past. Take my long-lost tail. You've got one too!

TAILBONE

TELL TAIL

Our ancestors lost their tails over twenty million years ago. When a baby is developing in the womb, it still has a tiny tail, but it disappears by the time it is born. The leftover bones form our coccyx, or tailbone.

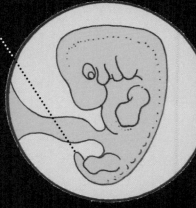

TINY TAIL ON A DEVELOPING BABY

MISSING MUSCLE

Hold out your arm, palm-side up, then touch your pinky finger to your thumb. Does a tendon pop up on your wrist? About ten percent of humans no longer have a **PALMARIS LONGUS** — a muscle that probably helped our ape ancestors climb trees.

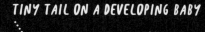

PALMARIS LONGUS

46

THRILLS AND CHILLS

When we are cold or scared, **GOOSEBUMPS** make tiny hairs on our skin stand up. Many animals make their fur or spines stand up to appear bigger to their enemies. Raised hairs also trap air, keeping furry animals warm. Humans are fur-free, so goosebumps are pretty pointless!

ARCTIC FOX KEEPING WARM

PORCUPINE FENDING OFF ATTACKERS

HUMAN GOOSEBUMPS

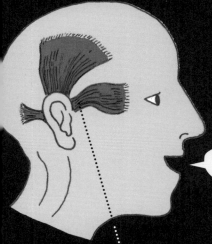

WALK!

AURICULAR MUSCLES UNDER THE SKIN

MANY ANIMALS CAN SWIVEL THEIR EARS TOWARDS SOUNDS

CAN YOU WIGGLE YOUR EARS?

We all have muscles to move our ears, but very few people are able to use them! **AURICULAR MUSCLES** are left over from when we were wild creatures. We would swivel our ears to listen out for danger.

EXTRA EYELID

BIRDS AND REPTILES HAVE THIS EYELID

LEFTOVER EYELID

The pink bit in the corner of your eye is the remains of an **EXTRA EYELID**. For many animals, a blink with this eyelid cleans the eye. When closed, it gives see-through protection, like built-in goggles. Pretty useful!

WEIRD AND WONKY EVOLUTION

AS HUMANS EVOLVED, SOME BODY PARTS GOT BIGGER AND OTHERS GOT SMALLER!

CROOKED TEETH

Many children need to have some adult **TEETH REMOVED** and others pulled into line. Most animals have straight teeth and our ancient ancestors had aligned canines. So what's up with our modern mouths?

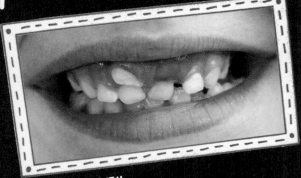

A CROWDED MOUTH

CHEESE!

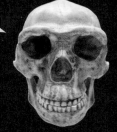

THIS ZEBRA HAS PERFECT TEETH.

AN EARLY HUMAN SKULL WITH STRAIGHT TEETH

BRACES STRAIGHTEN CROOKED TEETH

JAW BUSTING

It turns out that jaws grow with heavy use. Early humans gnawed **RAW MEAT** and chewed **TOUGH ROOTS**, which gave their jaws a workout.

Over time, we learned to grind grain and cook food. This **SOFT DIET** didn't need much chewing and our jaws slowly shrank. Now they are often too small to fit our teeth!

EARLY HUMANS HAD BIG JAWS

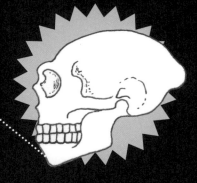

MODERN HUMANS HAVE SMALLER JAWS

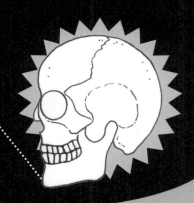

HUGE HEADS

Over millions of years, our **BRAIN** grew bigger, helping us to think up ways to survive. Our head grew to hold our bigger brain.

At the same time, our **PELVIS** got **NARROWER**, allowing us to walk tall on two legs.

OOPS!

Now a big-headed baby has to fit through a mom's narrow pelvis to be born!

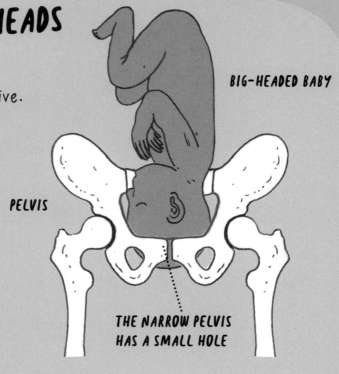

BIG-HEADED BABY

PELVIS

THE NARROW PELVIS HAS A SMALL HOLE

SQUEEZY SKULLS

Babies evolved so that five of the skull bones have gaps, called **FONTANELLES**, between. This allows the skull to mold and **SQUEEZE** through the pelvis. By the age of two, the skull bones have fused (joined) and the gaps are gone.

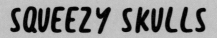

GAPS BETWEEN THE SKULL BONES

You were born with still-growing, partly bendy bones. Hard bones grow and fuse together as you get older. Most baby animals have a finished skeleton so they can stand and walk right away.

WE ARE ALL MUTANTS!

TINY CHANGES INSIDE THE BODY CAN LEAD TO **BIG** CHANGES FOR HUMANKIND.

NEED-TO-KNOW FACTS

GENES are instructions that build your body and tell it how to work. You inherit half of your genes from your biological parents. You have 20,000 genes in your body.

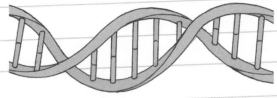

NORMAL GENE

MUTATED GENE: sometimes a gene can be changed, missing, or "broken." This mutant gene may be passed down from a parent to their children.

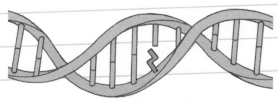

MUTATED GENE

FOR GENES, "MUTANT" MEANS CHANGED, NOT BAD OR MONSTROUS!

As humans evolved and multiplied, some **MUTATED GENES** were passed on through the generations and spread across the world. As a result, some things in our bodies work differently from the way they started out.

MUTANT GENES

DID YOU KNOW EXPLOSIVE POOP IS INHERITED?

YEAH, IT RUNS IN YOUR GENES!

For most humans, the ability to **DIGEST MILK** is "switched off" at the age of about five. After this, dairy foods can cause stomach pain — and explosive poop! So, why can some people still enjoy milk?

Around 10,000 years ago, some humans developed a mutated gene that keeps milk digestion "switched on." Now one third of people have this gene.

If you can drink milk (and you're older than five) then **YOU'RE A MILK-DRINKING MUTANT!**

Ever wondered why you need to eat fruits and veggies? One reason is that, unlike most animals, we don't make our own **VITAMIN C.** Long ago humans DID make vitamin C in their bodies, but a mutation "broke" the vitamin-C-producing gene. Our ancestors at the time ate plenty of vitamin-packed fruits, so they survived and passed on the mutant gene. **NOW WE ARE ALL VITAMIN DEPRIVED MUTANTS!**

If we don't get enough vitamin C, we can get scurvy — a nasty disease that makes your teeth fall out! Between the years 1400 and 1700, millions of people died of scurvy. It was common among sailors and pirates on voyages where there were no fresh fruits or veggies.

DATA DUMP

BAD MEDICINE

THROUGHOUT HISTORY, PEOPLE HAVE TRIED ALL SORTS OF STRANGE WAYS TO KEEP HEALTHY.

WARNING! DO NOT TRY ANY OF THESE TERRIBLE TREATMENTS AT HOME!

In the 1700s and 1800s, people thought it was possible to save victims of drowning by **BLOWING SMOKE UP THEIR BUTTS.** It was believed that the warm, dry fumes of tobacco smoke could get the heart and lungs of the drowned person working again.

Trepanning, or drilling **HOLES IN THE SKULL,** was practiced for thousands of years. This awful operation was used to treat head injuries, relieve pain, and even to pull evil spirits from the body.

From the Middle Ages until the 1700s, mummified bodies were stolen from ancient Egyptian tombs and ground up to create **MUMMY POWDER.** The powder was used in Europe to treat everything from eye infections to stomach troubles.

In the early 1900s, a radioactive chemical called radium was sold as a wonder cure. People drank **WATER INFUSED WITH RADIUM** for their health. Sadly, it was later discovered that radium causes cancer.

In Ancient Egypt, swallowing a spoonful of **SNAIL SLIME** was the soothing cure for a sore throat. Eye infections were treated with a drop of **BAT'S BLOOD**.

Bad medicine is not just something from the ancient past. Up until the 1950s, doctors recommended smoking cigarettes as a cure for sore throats and coughs. We now know that smoking causes cancer! Maybe some of the cures that we believe in now will seem bizarre in the future.

4,000 years ago in ancient Mesopotamia, if you ground your teeth at night the doctor would recommend **SLEEPING WITH A SKULL**. Patients were told to kiss and lick the skull seven times each night for a week!

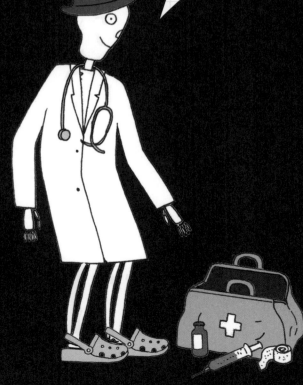

CAN YOU THINK YOURSELF BETTER?

PRETEND PILLS AND POTIONS CAN TRICK THE BRAIN INTO MAKING US FEEL BETTER.

YOU CAN'T TRICK ME!

NEED-TO-KNOW FACTS

When scientists make **NEW MEDICINES** for treating feelings like pain or nausea (feeling sick to your stomach), they need to be tested to make sure they work.

A test is set up where some patients are given the new medicine and others get a look-alike fake medicine, called a **PLACEBO** (say PLA-SEE-BOW). Only the doctors know which is which. Often patients feel better after taking the placebo!

I AM BEING LOOKED AFTER. I'M GOING TO FEEL BETTER

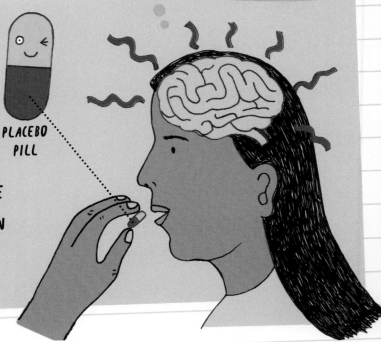

CLEVER TRICKS
For the brain to be tricked, everything needs to feel real.

✔ **PLACEBO LOOKS REALISTIC**

✔ **PLACEBO GIVEN IN A MEDICAL CLINIC**

✔ **PLACEBBO GIVEN BY A DOCTOR OR NURSE**

✔ **PATIENT IS GIVEN CARE AND ATTENTION**

PLACEBO PILL

- People **EXPECT** medicine to help make them feel better. This **BELIEF** is often enough to have a positive effect.

- After taking a placebo, the brain often makes its own pain-busting, feel-good chemicals: **ENDORPHINS**. They can make us feel better, a lot like real medicines.

DOCTOR! I HAVE A STRAWBERRY STUCK IN MY EAR!

DON'T WORRY I'VE GOT SOME CREAM FOR THAT.

CAN YOU BELIEVE IT?

What we believe can have a big effect on how we feel and behave.

FULL OF SURPRISES

Scientists gave two groups of people exactly the same milkshake. One group was told it was a basic shake, the other was told it was a creamy "super shake." The super shake group felt fuller. That's because their brains released more of the body chemical that tells us we're full.

BASIC SHAKE

SUPER SHAKE

I FEEL WIDE AWAKE!

TOP MARKS

Scientists have found that when people are tricked into thinking they have had an extra-long sleep, they feel more awake and get better grades on tests the next day!

Before modern medicines, belief was important for curing illness. The ancient Egyptians thought that a dead mouse could soothe a toothache, and because they believed in it, it probably helped!

FLIP BACK <<< to page 52 for more info about **CURIOUS CURES**

SPOOKY SENSATIONS

TRY THIS

SOMETIMES OUR BODY DOES ONE THING, WHILE OUR BRAIN DOES ANOTHER.

BRAINIAC HACK: SECRET SENSE

PROPRIOCEPTION is the sense that gives you an awareness of your body. Sensors in your muscles and joints send messages to the brain telling it where all the parts of your body are and whether they are moving.

COME ON!

I AM PUSHING AS HARD AS I CAN!

Proprioception helps us to know how hard or softly we are **PULLING** or **PUSHING**, and how much **EFFORT** is needed to do something.

DISAPPEARING FLOOR

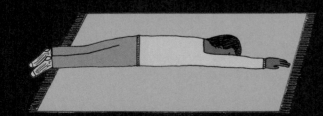

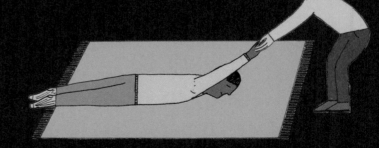

Lie face down on the floor with your arms above your head. Keep your eyes closed.

Get a friend to lift you by your arms until your head hangs down off the floor.

FLOATING ARMS

Stand in a doorway with the back of your hands against the frame. Push as hard as you can against the door frame for 30 seconds.

Step away from the door and relax your arms. They will slowly start to rise.

EXPLANATION:
After you tense your muscles to push your arms against the door frame, your brain continues to send a message to those muscles, even after you stop.

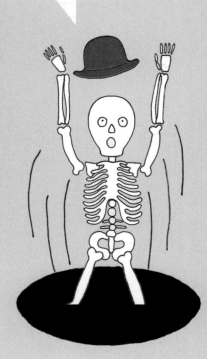

After 40 seconds, your friend lowers your arms slooowly back down. What do you feel?

EXPLANATION:
You have just confused your **PROPRIOCEPTION.** Your brain sends messages to the body telling it that it is already on the floor. When your friend lowers you down, it feels like you are going through the floor.

FLIP BACK <<< to page 18 for more about **PROPRIOCEPTION**

TRY THIS

GHOSTLY VISIONS

ARE YOUR EYES PLAYING TRICKS ON YOU? MAYBE . . .

BRAINIAC HACK: SIGHT CELLS

We see with two kinds of light-sensitive cells at the back of our eyes. **ROD CELLS** and **CONE CELLS**.

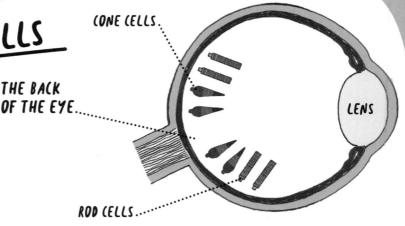

CONE CELLS

THE BACK OF THE EYE

LENS

ROD CELLS

ROD CELLS work in dim light.

ROD CELLS can pick out the **SHAPES** of things, even when it's really dark. They don't recognize colors, so we see everything in shades of gray.

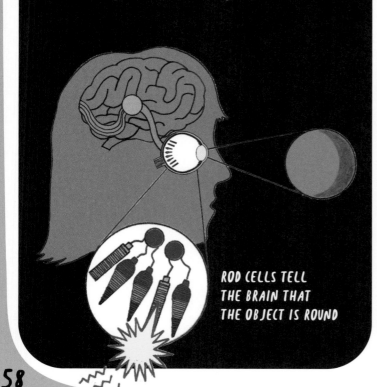

ROD CELLS TELL THE BRAIN THAT THE OBJECT IS ROUND

CONE CELLS work in bright light.

We see **COLORS** with **CONE CELLS**. Some cones detect **BLUE** light, some detect **GREEN**, and others **RED**. Their combined signals are sent to the brain, which allows us to see millions of colors.

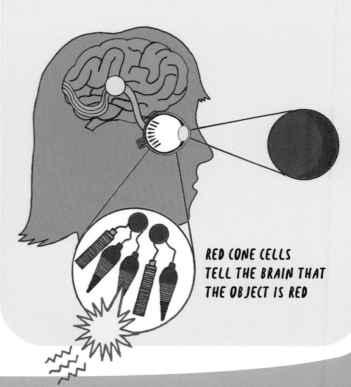

RED CONE CELLS TELL THE BRAIN THAT THE OBJECT IS RED

TRAPPING MONSTERS

Looking at one color for a while tires your **CONE CELLS** out!
Give your red cells a workout with this activity.

Stare at the red monster and count to 20. Then quickly look at the empty cage. What do you see?

EXPLANATION:

When you look at the red monster, your red cells have to work hard sending signals to your brain. After a while they get tired, so the green and blue cells take over. When you look away, you briefly see a spooky blue-green **AFTERIMAGE** created by the blue and green cone cells.

NIGHT VISION NINJA

Follow these tips regularly to get your night vision rod cells ready for action!

1. EAT SOME VEGGIES
Leafy veggies are packed with vitamin A, which helps to keep your eyes healthy.

2. DIM YOUR SCREENS
Looking at bright lights at any time makes it harder for your eyes to adjust to darkness.

3. SHADE YOUR EYES
Wear sunglasses or a sunhat to prevent bright sunlight from damaging your eyes.

GLOSSARY

BACTERIA
Very small life forms that are found everywhere and can cause diseases.

BILE
A bitter greenish-yellow fluid that helps the body to digest food.

CELLS
The body is made up of trillions of tiny cells which carry out different jobs in the body such as fighting germs and delivering food.

CARBOHYDRATES
Energy-giving substances found in foods such as bread, potatoes, pasta, and rice.

DIGESTIVE SYSTEM
The body parts that break down food and liquid so that they can be used by the body.

DISABILITY
An illness, injury, or condition that makes it difficult to do some things. A disability is usually permanent or lasts for a long time.

ESOPHAGUS
The muscular tube that connects the throat to the stomach.

EVOLUTION
The process by which living things changed and developed over millions of years.

GLAND
An organ that produces liquid chemicals for use in the body.

LARGE INTESTINE
The long, tube-like part of your digestive system where poop is formed.

MICROORGANISM
A living thing that can only be seen with a microscope.

MUCUS
A thick, slimy liquid produced inside the nose and other parts of the body.

NERVES
Long fibers that carry information to the brain from the senses and instructions from the brain to the body.

NEURON
A cell that carries information between parts of the brain and between the brain and other parts of the body.

ORGAN
A part of the body that does a particular job. The heart, lungs, and brain are all organs.

PELVIS
The large bony frame below the waist to which the leg bones and spine are joined.

RADIATION
A type of energy that is released in waves. Some kinds can be very dangerous to health.

RECTUM
A short tube that connects the large intestine with the anus—the opening where poop leaves the body.

SMALL INTESTINE
Part of the digestive system where nutrients from food are taken into the body.

SPINAL CORD
Nerves inside the spine that connect nearly all parts of the body to the brain.

VEIN
A tube that carries blood to the heart from the other parts of the body.

WOMB
The organ in which a baby develops before it is born.

GENDER WORDS

CISGENDER
When the gender identity we feel best describes us matches the sex we were assigned at birth.

GENITALS
The sexual organs outside the body (penis in a male and vagina in a female).

INTERSEX
Being born with a mixture of both female and male sexual organs.

NON-BINARY
When we feel somewhere inbetween "boy" or "girl." Or neither!

TRANSGENDER (or trans)
When the gender identity we feel best describes us does not match the sex we were assigned at birth.

WE WANT ANSWERS!

11 SUDOKU

2	1	3	4
4	3	1	2
3	2	4	1
1	4	2	3

2	1	3	4
4	3	1	2
1	2	4	3
3	4	2	1

33 HAPPY OR SAD?

The child on the left could be surprised, scared, or happy.

The child on the right could be shy, suspicious, or sad.

37 FAIR PLAY

The bottom scene has poor accessibility.
The top scene has good accessibility.

The six differences in the top scene are:
1. There are smooth paths. These are good for wheelchair users, people with mobility issues, and people with impaired sight.
2. There is a net swing. This is safe and easy for everyone to use.

3. There is a ramp over the stream. This is easy to walk or wheel across.
4. The drinking fountain has taps at different heights. This means water can be reached by lots of different park users.
5. Both of the flowerbeds are raised. This makes it possible for people with mobility issues to enjoy the flowers.
6. The picnic table has a space for a wheelchair.

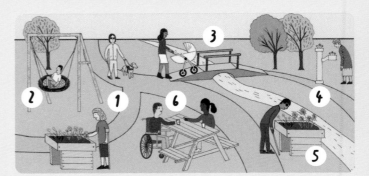

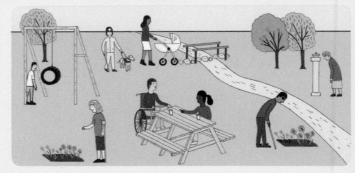

FIND OUT MORE . . .

https://www.genderbread.org

https://www.bbc.co.uk/cbbc/shows/operation-ouch

https://www.youtube.com/@besmart/playlists
("Evolution is amazing" and "Science of the human body")

https://www.sciencemuseum.org.uk/objects-and-stories/science-and-technology-medicine
https://www.sciencemuseum.org.uk/objects-and-stories/understanding-body

https://kids.frontiersin.org/articles/neuroscience-and-psychology

INDEX

ROSIE COOPER

is a London-based user researcher, originally from New Zealand. She had eight teeth extracted as a child and still wears a retainer at night. Her speediest poopcorn journey is around 14 hours. Sadly, she cannot wiggle her ears.

HARRIET RUSSELL

is the illustrator of over ten books for children including the bestselling *This Book Thinks You're a Scientist* published by Thames & Hudson. She lives in rural West Sussex.

STEVE PARKER

is an award-winning nature and science expert who has written and edited over 70 books on the human body for a range of readerships. He has worked at London's Natural History Museum and is a Scientific Fellow of the Zoological Society of London.

The Brainiac's Book of the Body and Brain © 2024 Thames & Hudson Ltd, London
Text © 2024 Rosie Cooper
Illustrations © 2024 Harriet Russell

Edited by Catherine Ard
Designed by Belinda Webster
Scientific consultant Steve Parker

First published in the United States of America in 2024 by Thames & Hudson Inc., 500 Fifth Avenue, New York, New York 10110

Library of Congress Control Number 2023935732

ISBN 978-0-500-65245-9

Printed and bound in China by RR Donnelley

FSC
www.fsc.org

MIX
Paper | Supporting
responsible forestry
FSC® C144853

Be the first to know about our new releases, exclusive content and author events by visiting
thamesandhudson.com
thamesandhudson usa.com
thamesandhudson.com.au

Photography credits
a = above; b = below; c = center; l = left; r = right

page 8: Cultural Creative R/Alamy
page 14: Kai Keisuke/Shutterstock
page 15: (donut) Chones/Shutterstock
page 15: (ice cream) Pics five/Shutterstock
page 15: (flower) BoxerX/Shutterstock
page 15: (lemon) Purple Clouds/Shutterstock
page 15: (chocolate) Natapob/Shutterstock
page 15: (leaf) Nataly Studio/Shutterstock
page 15: (bracelet) Tanya_Terekhina/Shutterstock
page 15: (key) Michal Vitek/Shutterstock
page 15: (robot) okonart/Shutterstock
page 15: (ladybird) Irin-K/Shutterstock
page 15: (button) Pics five/Shutterstock
page 15: (straw) xpixel/Shutterstock
page 24l: New Africa/Shutterstock
page 24c: GoodFocused/Shutterstock
page 30: nobeastsofierce
page 33l: karelnoppe/Shutterstock
page 33r: pathdoc/Shutterstock
page 35: Artefact/Alamy
page 38r: INTERFOTO/Alamy
page 38l: Zvonimir Atletic/Shutterstock
page 39bl: World History Archive/Alamy
page 39ar: Chris Hellier/Alamy
page 39al: Janaka Dharmasena/Shutterstock
page 40: Phanie/Alamy
page 41bl: Museum of Radiation and Radioactivity, Oakridge Associated University Museum
page 41ac: Mikhail Reshetnikov/Alamy
page 41br: GagliardiPhotography/Shutterstock
page 41bc: Triff/Shutterstock
page 47cr: teekayu/Shutterstock
page 47al: maik555/Shutterstock
page 47ar: Oksana Stasenko/Shutterstock
page 47bl: DenisNata/Shutterstock
page 47br: Ian Dyball/Shutterstock
page 48cl: Galovtsik Gabor/Shutterstock
page 48c: creativemarc/Shutterstock
page48ra: Charise Wilson/Shutterstock
page 48cr: Robert Przybysz/Shutterstock
page 48ar: 48ar: Charise Wilson/Shutterstock
page 51: Sonsedska Yuliia/Shutterstock
page 52ar: Joseph Jacques de Gardane/Wellcome
page 52bl: Science History Images/Alamy
page 53al: Aleksandar Dickov/Shutterstock
page 53bl: Nathapol Kongseang/Shutterstock

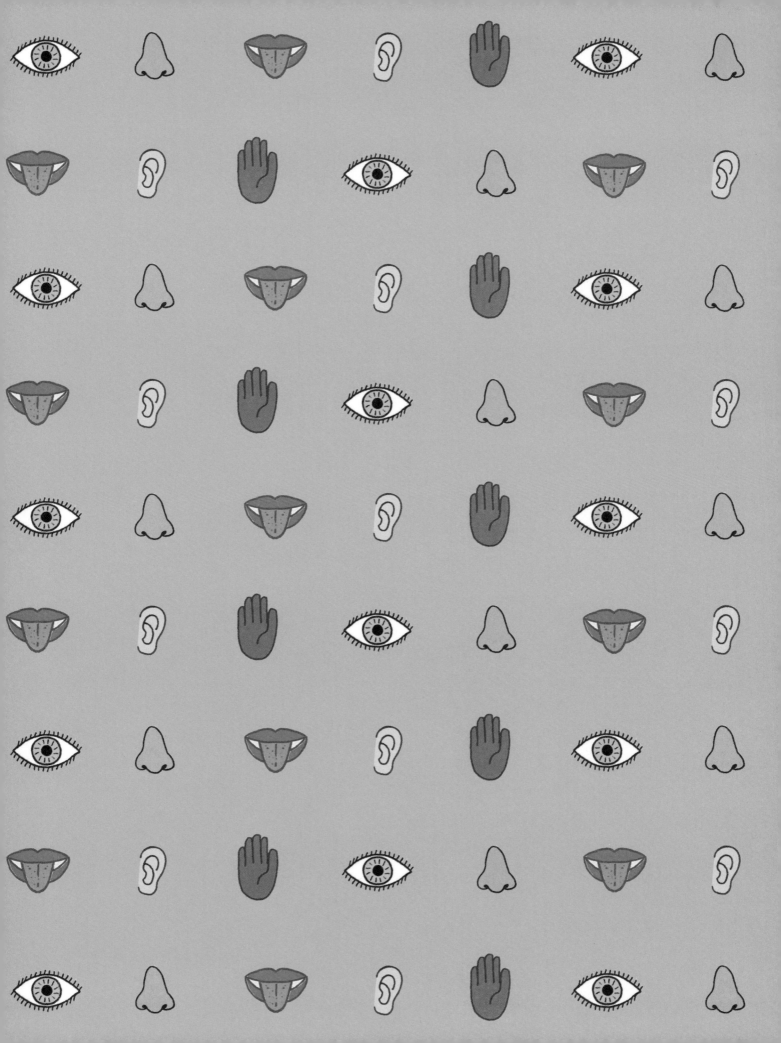